Bad Fairies

Bad Fairies

The real reason for the bad stuff that happens in life

Fay Langmore

BARRON'S

First edition for the United States,
its territories and possessions, and Canada published in 2004 by
Barron's Educational Series, Inc.
by arrangement with
the Ivy Press Limited

All inquiries should be addressed to:
Barron's Educational Series, Inc.,
250 Wireless Boulevard
Hauppauge, New York 11788
www.barronseduc.com

International Standard Book Number
0-7641-5702-7

Library of Congress Catalog Card No. 2003112243

This book was conceived,
designed, and produced by
THE IVY PRESS LIMITED
The Old Candlemakers
West Street, Lewes
East Sussex, BN7 2NZ, U.K.

Creative Director **Peter Bridgewater**
Publisher **Sophie Collins**
Editorial Director **Steve Luck**
Design Manager **Tony Seddon**
Senior Project Editor **Rebecca Saraceno**
Designers **Clare Barber, Tonwen Jones**
Illustrator **Tonwen Jones**
Picture Research **Vanessa Fletcher**

Printed in China
9 8 7 6 5 4 3 2 1

Contents

Introduction

Fairies—they're those pretty little things that are supposed to live at the bottom of the garden, aren't they? Flitting about among the flowers in lacy little outfits, waving their wands and casting spells to make life nice for us human folk? If that's what you think, you're in for a real shock. Okay, there are some kind-hearted fairy folk who fit that description, with diaphanous wings and sparkly dresses, but they are in the minority.

In fact, the Good Fairies are outnumbered almost two to one by the Bad Fairies, and this little book is a guide to the various forms of mischief they get up to. While the Good Fairies flutter around our human world bringing joy and happiness, there is a task force of Bad Fairies making sure that they are facing an uphill struggle. Their sole aim in life is to inject

mayhem and misery into our lives. So, if you ever wondered why the whole world seems against you sometimes, or were looking for somebody to blame for your woes and shortcomings, this is where to look. At last, here's an explanation for all life's little annoyances—they are brought about by an army of fairies, goblins, sprites, trolls, and the like, lying in ambush for us unsuspecting human punching bags.

They're pretty well organized, too, dividing the workload according to their many and various skills. There also exists the equivalent of Bad Fairy Trade Unions—ancient Guilds that protect their workers and pass on age-old crafts to younger generations.

These cover many fields of mischief-making, ranging from the simply annoying right through to the positively life-threatening, and there is a long-standing tradition of cooperation between Guilds to guarantee maximum havoc to our lives.

Although the stereotypical view of fairies is based on the more common "Good Fairy" model, there is evidence in the folklore of many cultures that we are aware of the Bad Fairies, too. But, surprisingly little research has been done into the subject until now. In the modern world of scientific discovery, it seems we are more easily persuaded that the things that keep going wrong in our lives are caused by inexorable laws of physics, chemistry, or probability. Current thinking would have us believe that dropped toast lands butter-side down nine times out of ten due to aerodynamics and the different weight of the two sides of the toast—but let's be honest, most of us suspect there are other, more malign forces at work here.

So, this book is an attempt to give some insight into the workings of this murky underworld of mischievous goings-on, and a guide to the organizations that it seems we are powerless to oppose. It's not an exhaustive study, nor will it actually help you to deal with the glitches that keep on happening, but it might just make you feel slightly better to know that many things are really not your fault. And don't for one second believe that myth that a fairy dies every time someone says they don't believe in fairies. This causes endless sniggers and amusement down in the fairy taverns, where they don't believe that humans are masters of their own destiny. So, please don't give these Bad Fairies the satisfaction of amusing themselves!

The Shit Happens Fairies

*F*or most of us there is only one law—Murphy's Law—if something can go wrong, it will. The classic example is Dropped Toast Syndrome: if you fumble with your breakfast, it's bound to end up butter-side down, but not only that—nine times out of ten it'll land in the dustiest corner of the room.

Some people just shrug their world-weary shoulders and sigh, "That's life," and others seek to find scientific explanations, but the truth is actually much more simple. Yes, there is such a thing as Murphy's Law, but it isn't just a law of nature. It was formulated by a convention of Fairy Folk many moons ago, and the Shit Happens Fairies were appointed as official law enforcers.

The élite of the Bad Fairy community are the ones that strike most frequently, often only in small ways, to turn a good day sour or transform the opportunity of a lifetime into an experience you'll never forget. They ply their wicked trade through various devious means, making sure the world doesn't live up to our expectations.

AFFILIATION
Ex officio members of all
major Guilds

MOST ACTIVE
Among hopeless optimists

TEMPERAMENT
Gleeful and contrary,
of course

The Three Gleeful Sisters of Contrariness

Psyche, Putrida, and Peryl (or Mad, Bad, and Dangerous, as they're affectionately known) are the flying squad of the Bad Fairy underworld. They outrank all the other Shit Happens Fairies, and have a hand in just about any horror the Little People drop us into, without directly creating mayhem themselves. Their main task is to make sure that hopes and expectations are frustrated one way or another—not only by instilling a ludicrous sense of optimism in their victims, but also by ensuring that just the right kind of misfortune comes our way. Their powers of communication and logistics are honed to perfection, gathering intelligence from all the Fairy Guilds and then mobilizing the most appropriate fairy fiend to cause a worst-case scenario. Not content with dashing the hopes of millions every day at the racetrack or slot machines (humdrum stuff), these girls delight in complex scams that result in dates from hell, the backfiring money-making scheme, or the vacation you need a holiday to get over.

You better believe it! With precision timing, the gleeful gals will ensure you miss your vital connection by mere seconds.

13

AFFILIATION
The Noble Order of
Meteorological Fairies

MOST ACTIVE
Whenever we leave the house

TEMPERAMENT
Changeable

Weather Pixies

Don't be fooled by the authority of the meteorologists, they are just as much under the malign influence of the fairies as the rest of us. That's why their forecasts are so often spectacularly wrong. It doesn't matter how carefully you've checked the weather report or taken the advice of the old wives' tales... you know you're going to be ill-prepared for whatever the heavens can throw at you. All ready for the snow and ice, you set out from home into (you guessed it) stifling heat. Left home without your umbrella? It's bound to rain. And of course there are some scheming Little People to blame— the Weather Pixies. These mischief-makers are a motley bunch, ranging from the hot-tempered Sunshine Sprites and the gloomy Downpour Dwarves to the cold-hearted Frost Fairies. So, next time you're out and about and you think the weathermen have messed up again, think twice!

Lightning lookout...
With the Weather Pixies hard at work, are you willing to bet it won't strike twice?

15

AFFILIATION
Board member of the Guild of the Pixies of Perdition

MOST ACTIVE
Just before carpools, meetings, flights, deadlines

TEMPERAMENT
Nervous; can be soothed with quiet words and a firm grip

Translocation Fairy

Somewhere in the fairy world there is a repository for everything collected by this mischievous creature, where you can find (meticulously classified and cataloged) all the single socks, ballpoint pens, umbrellas, and house keys that you thought were lost forever. The Translocation Fairy, working on information from the Bad Timing Elves, ensures that just when you need it most, that all-important report will be nowhere to be found, and your credit card, which you always keep in your purse in that little compartment, just ain't there any more. She not only stores all that purloined plunder, but on occasion creates further havoc by returning things at inopportune moments...like the underwear that went missing from the laundry basket turns up in your briefcase at a business lunch, or vice versa, your misplaced, half-eaten sandwich turns up in your laundry basket.

Have you seen my... ?
Your house keys are safely stored here along with Grandma's dentures.

AFFILIATION
*Founding members of the
Guild of the Pixies of Perdition*

MOST ACTIVE
In times of need

TEMPERAMENT
*Melancholic, generally
at a loss*

The Pixies of Perdition

These children of the Translocation Fairy are the sad little fellers responsible for all lost things. Unlike the victims of their mother's interventions, the things they tamper with are not just misplaced, but usually lost forever. It's not just tangible stuff such as socks, pencils, or tools, but also things like telephone numbers, or your place in the book you've been struggling to finish. They're also responsible for the loss of hearts, hope, causes, direction, memory, sense of proportion, and sometimes, even the will to live. Trouble is, they seem to have lost their sense of humor, too, and take no joy in their work. A breakaway group, calling themselves the Negligence Gnomes, has been formed to bridge the gap between the Pixies of Perdition and Procrastinata. Although their primary function is to make sure things simply don't get done, they are still classified as the Pixies of Perdition.

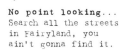

No point looking... Search all the streets in Fairyland, you ain't gonna find it.

19

AFFILIATION
Founding member of the Union of Regret-inducing Goblins

MOST ACTIVE
When you think the world is your oyster

TEMPERAMENT
Not exactly pessimistic, more long-suffering

Hindsight Hobgoblin

How often do you end up saying "it seemed a good idea at the time," just after experiencing the consequences of a mind-numbingly stupid decision? It's at that "Doh!" moment when the Hindsight Hobgoblin sitting on your shoulder starts rubbing his hands with glee. His initial spadework digs the hole you're about to throw yourself into, tempting you closer and closer to the brink until, supremely confident, you plunge in with both feet and discover the meaning of "deep in the doodoo." Messages whispered in your ear run along the lines of "Of course you don't need an electrician to do that rewiring," "Have you ever thought of taking up skydiving in your retirement?," "That looks like a really good investment," "He seems like just the right guy for the job," or simply "Why not?" Of course, once the deed is done, your embarrassment (and his excited pleasure) are almost endlessly prolonged by the torturous mental replays and your agonized "If only"s.

Artist's impression...
...of the spreading pools of anguish caused by this goblin's troublesome antics.

21

AFFILIATION
Society for the Promotion of Pointless Expenditure

MOST ACTIVE
Around the nouveau pauvre

TEMPERAMENT
Cool, calm, and collecting your last penny

HABITAT
The shopping mall,
the ATM

CHARACTER
Seductive, smooth-talking,
and irresistible

KNOWN ASSOCIATIONS
Gadget Gnomes, Hindsight
Hobgoblin

Shopping Siren

With a seductive voice that you just can't ignore, the Shopping Siren disingenuously lures you to the store, catalog or website that is least appropriate to your needs and bank balance. She can be heard loudest when your overdraft is at its limit, or when you've just lost your main source of income, and the only cure for the depression is retail therapy. She doesn't just encourage you to go out there and spend, spend, spend—oh no—this baby's smarter than that. You might get something practical, for heaven's sake! So she'll call in her associates, the Gadget Gnomes, to find something suitably useless and/or tasteless to send you deeper into dept, and then she'll call the Hindsight Hobgoblin to gloat. Don't think you can outsmart her by resisting the urge to buy stuff you don't need—even if you are careful to make only the most pragmatic purchase, you'll get home to find it's something you've already bought and forgotten about (and is probably the wrong size anyway), or your partner has just bought you as a present. Or, you'll discover that you could have found it in the shop next door at half the price.

CHAPTER TWO

The Bodily Function Fairies

F or every person who boasts that his or her body is a temple, there are dozens of the rest of us who are the not-so-proud owners of a run-down nonconformist chapel. Even those of us who actually do all the workouts and yogic contortions can't really, hand on heart, swear that they are in control of their magnificent physiques. Who are they trying to kid? I'll bet even Mr. Universe gets the gas.

Let's face it, our bodies are seldom to be relied upon, except to let us down at crucial moments. Some things are involuntary, such as sneezing; but other bodily functions are just not acceptable, probably because we mistakenly believe we have some control over them. Fat chance.

Unfortunately, these tend to be the more annoying, disgusting, and embarrassing foibles of our all-too-human frames, and they have a tendency to manifest themselves at the most inopportune moments. Of course, it's the Little People who are behind all this, and the pesky imps who are really in control are the Bodily Function Fairies. Working tirelessly day and night, they subtly influence our capacity for continence and physical well-being, making sure we let ourselves down in company, or suffer agonies of pain or embarrassment with all-too-common and sometimes trivial complaints.

AFFILIATION
Amalgamated Guild of Fairy
Youth Organizations

MOST ACTIVE
Around teenagers, or anybody
trying to make an impression

TEMPERAMENT
Sullen, bloody-minded

HABITAT
Bathrooms, rooms with mirrors

CHARACTER
Irritating, and sometimes even hurtful

KNOWN ASSOCIATIONS
Partypooper Fairy, Puck and Time-of-Your-Life Fairies

Zitania

Planning a really hot date? You guessed it—say hello to a volcano on the verge of eruption right in the middle of your face. Invitation to meet the family for dinner? Allergic rash from eating the seafood starter. Vitally important presentation to the Public Health and Hygiene committee? Instant ugly cold sore. Funeral? A blizzard of dandruff that sets off black beautifully. Zitania's to blame, of course, as she is with any sudden and highly visible changes to your complexion, but try explaining that to your prospective life partner, in-laws, or boss! In addition to embarrassing the hell out of you in front of your nearest and dearest, or dashing any chance you had of promotion, she's pretty good at making you physically uncomfortable too. That boil on your butt is going to give you an unforgettable long-haul flight to your vacation destination, and you can bet your bottom dollar your swimwear won't cover it.

Magnifying mirror
Zitania's absolute favorite tool to use against you.

27

AFFILIATION
*High Banshee of the Bodily
Function Fairies' Guild*

MOST ACTIVE
*Evenings, weekends, vacations,
hot dates, catered functions*

TEMPERAMENT
*Sophisticated, always appears
well behaved on first meeting*

HABITAT
Kitchen, grocery store, refrigerator, hot car, hands

CHARACTER
Seductive, a femme fatale (sometimes literally)

KNOWN ASSOCIATIONS
Bad Timing Elves, the Shit Happens Fairies

Partypooper Fairy

So, you're having a party, eh? Well—remember that startling projectile vomit that George Bush Sr. managed at his Japanese host's table? It could happen to you, courtesy of the Partypooper Fairy. She's pretty active with the biochemistry set in your kitchen to provide more after-dinner entertainment than you'd bargained for, but she can also put a hex on the do before it even starts. Working with various other Bodily Function Fairies, she ensures your kids, pets, or spouse will come down with a severe case of the runs half an hour before your guests arrive, and can simultaneously engineer an unwelcome visit from that manic depressive you met on vacation who just won't stop talking about his pitiful sex life. So basically, all the things you pray won't happen before a gathering you've been looking forward to for ages will happen, and you'll have the Partypooper Fairy to thank for it.

Not looking good?
The herpes virus is just one thing on the list of things you can get before your party.

AFFILIATION
President of the Bodily
Function Fairies' Guild

MOST ACTIVE
Around people of a certain age

TEMPERAMENT
Sly and spiteful

HABITAT
The more disgusting
anatomical parts

CHARACTER
Unpleasant and
unprepossessing

KNOWN ASSOCIATIONS
All Bodily Function Fairies and
Time-of-Your-Life Fairies

Puck

Okay, let's just get it out in the open—certain bodily functions afflict us all from time to time, and there's no getting away from it. If only there were… Puck is the sprite responsible for the unmentionable (in polite company) disruptions to our digestive and sexual well-being. I mean, this is the really embarrassing stuff. He can let you off lightly with a barely audible belly gurgle or hiccup at an inopportune moment, but is more likely to tempt you into thinking you can get away with a silent expulsion of gas at one end or the other—and then inflict a belch like a foghorn, or the mother and father of all posterior blasts, usually during a lull in conversation. Or, even worse, he might visit in the middle of what might politely be called an "intimate moment." That's assuming he allows you such a moment, when the main protagonist can rise to the occasion and not let himself down too soon, neither party gets cramps, and the performance is not greeted with loud snoring. That's Puck for you. But with a name like that, what do you expect?

31

AFFILIATION
Amalgamated Union of
Cosmetic Sprites

MOST ACTIVE
Overnight, after the shower

TEMPERAMENT
Painstaking and patient

HABITAT
Bedrooms and bathrooms

CHARACTER
Complex and unfathomable

KNOWN ASSOCIATIONS
Time-of-Your-Life Fairies

Bad Hairies

It should be our crowning glory, but for most of us, most of the time, our hair is just another one of those things with a mind of its own. Bad Hairies are in charge, and do their utmost to give us a bad hair day every day. If you want it straight, it'll be curly. If you want it wavy, no matter how much you pay, a perm will only last a matter of hours.

Working tirelessly at night with their curling tongs and frizzers, what a tangled web they weave for us to wake up to. Half of it will come out (painfully) in the brush, and the rest will veer alarmingly to one side of a crooked part—except for that one tuft that resolutely sticks up in an odd place, no matter what you do to stick it down.

If you're a gal, this is bad enough, but if you're a boy... boy, have you got problems. Forget euphemisms like "high forehead" or "wide parting"; the truth is you're losing it. The plucky little Bad Hairies have been at work with their tweezers. Is there anything to keep it in? You could try a small box. Otherwise, just enjoy all that extra hair they've cultivated sprouting from your nose, ears, and eyebrows.

Luscious locks...
... too bad for you that they're on your back.

AFFILIATION
Dental Division of the Bad
Fairy Medical Association

MOST ACTIVE
During times of stress

TEMPERAMENT
Dark and moody

HABITAT
In sweet or cold drinks and foods

CHARACTER
Sadistic, no redeeming features

KNOWN ASSOCIATIONS
Time-of-Your-Life Fairies, Bad Timing Elves, Insomnia

Bad Tooth Fairy

Remember the Tooth Fairy that used to come and give you cash for your baby teeth? Pretty soon it's going to be payback time. Her counterpart is the Bad Tooth Fairy, and she's a real sweetheart. Sweet enough to rot your teeth, and then use her formidable array of enamel-chipping and nerve-exposing tools to explore the decay!

Like all Bad Fairies, she can make her presence felt at any time, but prefers to choose her moments carefully. Weekends and holidays are prime time, of course, but late night will do in a pinch, and let's be honest, there's never a good time for bad teeth. She can be quite subtle in the range of discomfort she inflicts—from simple halitosis to the dull ache you just know is going to get worse, sudden jabs of sensitivity to iced drinks, or a full-blown, can't-think-of-anything-else, raging toothache that leaves you incapable of eating, mumbling incoherently, and generally a dribbling wreck.

A dribbling wreck
With swollen gums and an aching tooth, you'll be in agony from this Bad Tooth Fairy.

AFFILIATION
Chartered Society of Pixie
Psychology

MOST ACTIVE
At social gatherings,
in families

TEMPERAMENT
Volatile, highly dangerous

HABITAT
*Around adolescents, but
can attack anybody*

CHARACTER
Mean and moody

KNOWN ASSOCIATIONS
*Road Rage Goblins,
Robin Badfellow*

Moodshifting Meanies

There's a small battalion of malevolent little sprites who wait until you're in a particularly contented frame of mind, then plunge you suddenly, for no apparent reason, into depression, rage, unsociability, cruelty, and crankiness. No apparent reason? Oh come on, they know what they're doing—these mood swings aren't just to make you feel bad; they really get other people's backs up too.

Without warning, there's no more Mr. Nice Guy, just a sad, lonely old grouch who irritates the hell out of anyone who comes near. Your friends just can't do or say anything right as far as you're concerned— and they can't understand why you're being such a sourpuss. In addition to ruining any cheerful atmosphere and trying the patience of even the sunniest personality, Moodshifting Meanies use their wicked sense of humor to good effect on more somber occasions, too. Who else could make you uncontrollably giggly in a library, or irrepressibly cheerful at a funeral?

In a serious state?
The Meanies can play
your serotonin levels
like a piano...always
at the wrong times.

37

AFFILIATION
Secretary of the Association of Nocturnal Fairy Operatives

MOST ACTIVE
In the dead of night

TEMPERAMENT
Dark and dreadful, unforgiving

HABITAT
Bedrooms, hotel rooms, and
night flights

CHARACTER
Melancholic and gloomy

KNOWN ASSOCIATIONS
Creaking Floorboard Banshee,
Alarm Afreet

Insomnia

At the end of a long, hard day, there's nothing like a good night's sleep.
And that's exactly what you're going to get—nothing like a good night's
sleep. You'll toss and turn miserably until dawn, eventually losing
consciousness, exhausted, about five minutes before the alarm goes off.
Another successful night for Insomnia.

Remember the Princess and the pea? Who do you think was
behind all that? That's right, Insomnia, controller of broken
bed springs and animated bedclothes, instiller of
nocturnal doubts, fears, and worries, and inventor
of the slowing-down clock. Her aim in life is
to make sure we greet each new day looking
dreadful, feeling worse, and hardly able to keep
our eyes open. If you do manage to cheat her
by grabbing a few hours sleep, beware! She's
picked up a trick or two from her sister Mab,
the Queen of the Night, who brings dreams
to the human world. Just as you finally
nod off, Insomnia will deliver a corker of a
nightmare—one that'll have you sitting bolt
upright, bug-eyed and sweating—that'll stop
you from doing it again any time soon.

Moon madness
Priding herself on her
feminine unpredictability,
she's sometimes much worse
during a full moon.

CHAPTER THREE

The Darkside Division

For every good fairy that we know about, there is a darkside counterpart. This Darkside Division is responsible for making sure that for every good thing that happens, there's a disaster just around the corner; for every good intention we have, there's a false expectation; and for every good day, there's going to be a week of absolute stinkers.

They're often related to their Good Fairy equivalents and they look almost as sweet, but don't be fooled—the family resemblance is merely superficial. Where their sisters and cousins sprinkle joy in their magic dust, these guys spread the misery with a trowel. As always in the Bad Fairy world, for them the essential ingredient for a successful mission is the timing—what could be merely a temporary blip under normal circumstances becomes a gale-force catastrophe in the hands of a skillful Darkside worker. And what could be more effective than following in the footsteps of their benevolent relations, undoing all the sweetness and light with a few well-aimed flicks of a Darkside wand? Next time you're granted three wishes by a friendly fairy, make sure your third is "I wish I hadn't asked for the first two," or you might end up dealing with the Darkside.

AFFILIATION
Grand Matriarch of the
Charitable Bad Fairy Sorority

MOST ACTIVE
In maternity hospitals,
nurseries, etc

TEMPERAMENT
Unflappable and matronly

HABITAT
Registrars' offices; the births,
marriages, and obituary pages

CHARACTER
Generous and kindly, attentive

KNOWN ASSOCIATIONS
All Bodily Function Fairies,
Tourette's Troll, Procrastinata

The Fairy Badmother

She's the uninvited guest at every newborn's welcoming party, bestowing her gifts generously on each and every one of us... and these presents are made to last. Not content with the usual silver baby spoons, miniature bracelets and toys that we'll either grow out of or lose in time, she has a fabulous store of everlasting and intangible gifts, from which she carefully chooses the most appropriate.

It's her we have to blame for all our irksome and ineradicable little characteristics that irritate our nearest and dearest and embarrass us until our dying days. Maybe it's just a tendency to be late for everything, or to squeeze the toothpaste from the middle of the tube. Or, it could be a little mannerism: say, a nervous cough. Perhaps she's given you the inability to say anything without adding an annoying cliché, or the habit of finishing everybody's sentences for them. Whatever, it's all thanks to your Fairy Badmother.

Perfectly gorgeous... and guaranteed some particularly close attention from the Fairy Badmother.

AFFILIATION
Chair, Chartered Society of
Pixie Psychology

MOST ACTIVE
At parties, weddings, bars,
diplomatic summits

TEMPERAMENT
Insufferably exuberant

Robin Badfellow

In a way, this guy's just like his cousin Robin Goodfellow. He likes to make sure that every convivial gathering goes with a swing—but the difference is, it could just as easily be a left hook followed by an uppercut to the jaw if our Darkside imp has anything to do with it. He's a real party animal and likes nothing better than to flit from bar to party to formal do, sowing seeds of discontent. Whenever there's a celebration of friendship, camaraderie, or a meeting of minds, Robin B. gets to work. Suspicion, misunderstandings, and antagonism are his trademarks, and parties soon turn from hugs and handshakes to rows and ructions, and a chat over a beer can spell the end of a lifelong friendship. Turning the conversation from jolly small talk to a flaming argument within minutes, Robin guarantees the whole thing will end in tears.

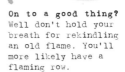

On to a good thing?
Well don't hold your breath for rekindling an old flame. You'll more likely have a flaming row.

AFFILIATION
The Guild of Elvish Delivery
and Journeymen

MOST ACTIVE
Christmas, birthdays

TEMPERAMENT
Childish and giggly

HABITAT
Under fir trees, in mail boxes

CHARACTER
Industrious and well-organized

KNOWN ASSOCIATIONS
Robin Badfellow, Bad Timing Elves, Translocation Fairy

Satan's Little Helpers

A small army of dwarves—the Darkside counterparts of Santa's Little Helpers, the elves who assist Saint Nicholas in his preparations for the festive season—work all year round assisting Old Nick in his work. Strangely, you can't help liking their ingenious (but puerile) sense of humor.

Of course, the high point of their year is Christmas, when they can mix up the labels on the presents so that the primmest of your elderly aunts gets that hilarious illustrated sex manual, and your partner gets the tasteless knitted tea cosy, but they don't stop there. Any occasion for the giving of gifts or sending of cards is a golden opportunity. Valentine's Day? A card in the wrong envelope will guarantee disruption to your love life. New baby? Obviously, you send that "In deepest sympathy" card. Birthday? How many loud ties can a man need? The list goes on...

Christmas gifts
A gesture of goodwill can be turned into a devilish present.

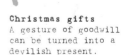

AFFILIATION
Honorary member of the Guild of the Bodily Function Fairies

MOST ACTIVE
When you thought you could get away with it

TEMPERAMENT
Quiet, unassuming, but assertive

HABITAT
In confined spaces and
public transport

CHARACTER
Furtive, secretive, and
underhand

KNOWN ASSOCIATIONS
The Bodily Function Fairies—
especially Puck

Stinkerbell

The fairy featured in "Peter Pan" is a pretty, frail little
creature, worried that her existence is threatened by children's
disbelief in fairies. Altogether more robust is her aunt
Stinkerbell, who doesn't really give a damn what people
think of her—she knows they are only too aware of the effects she has.

By casting her spell on foodstuffs such as garlic and gorgonzola,
or cooking up antidotes to soap, deodorant, and mouthwash, she turns
the person next to you into an olfactory nightmare.
Thanks to her, you'll get a blast of the Halitosis
Chorus from the feller next to you on the plane,
or find your face at straphanger's armpit height
in the rush-hour subway, or discover at the
local gym that trench foot isn't confined to the
trenches. But worst of all, by the subtle use of
beans, curries, and various vegetables, Stinkerbell
can create a human time bomb, due to go off in
front of you in the elevator. And, everybody
else will suspect that it's you!

Little stinker
Guaranteed to be
chopped so finely you
won't see it coming.

49

AFFILIATION
Bad Fairy Representative on
the Board of Flower Fairies

MOST ACTIVE
When you're trying to think of
something else

TEMPERAMENT
Constant and loyal

Forget-Me-Not

Unusual for the Darkside Division, Forget-Me-Not has counterparts not only in the world of benevolent flower fairies, but also contrary relatives in the Bad Fairy community. She's second cousin to both Amnesia and Aphasia, whose job it is to impair our memories, but her purpose is exactly the opposite, as her name suggests.

If you've just had a nightmare (thanks to her colleague Insomnia), she'll stimulate those little gray memory cells so it stays with you all day. Another favorite prank of hers is to present you with a ghastly image on the TV news that haunts you for hours, or assail your senses with a terrible taste or nasty smell you can't get rid of. Her most effective trick, though, is her simplest and the most maddening: on the radio, or in the supermarket, you hear the most inane and irritating tune (the title of which will of course elude you), and then you catch yourself humming the wretched thing for at least a week.

Tasteless tunes
Choose a station carefully, because you'll be singing that tune all week.

51

AFFILIATION
*Has not filed any application
for Guild membership—yet*

MOST ACTIVE
*At the eleventh hour
—or later*

TEMPERAMENT
Easy-going, devil-may-care

Procrastinata

Here is another one of the Darkside fairies who works so subtly, sugaring the pill of panic by instilling in us a false sense of security. Procrastinata can actually make us glow with the feeling that there's plenty of time left to do what you need to do, so no need to hurry—why not just relax and enjoy a little more leisure time before getting on with it? She does this by stretching time like elastic, and just at the last minute letting it snap back, with a startling effect.

Deadlines are a prime target, naturally. Like a reverse telescope, she can make them seem miles away, until the sudden sickening realization that it's actually too late to finish the job in time. And you know deep down that she's behind your stupid decision to put off dealing with the dripping faucet/faulty light switch/squeaky brakes—not to mention renewing the insurance policy—until disaster forces your hand.

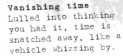

Vanishing time
Lulled into thinking you had it, time is snatched away, like a vehicle whizzing by.

53

AFFILIATION
Spokesperson for the Guild of
Fairy Communication Workers

MOST ACTIVE
When your mind is on
something else

TEMPERAMENT
Quick-thinking and cunning

HABITAT
Cocktail parties, business meetings, diplomatic summits

CHARACTER
Mischievous and disobedient

KNOWN ASSOCIATIONS
Slip o' the Tongue, Bad Timing Elves, Will o' the Whispers

Tourette's Troll

What is it that makes us so conscious of somebody's most prominent feature that we can't help drawing attention to it at every opportunity? Okay, so that woman we met out shopping has a big nose, but why did we have to go on about sniffing out a bargain? And we **know** the guy in the wheelchair wouldn't make a good stand-up comedian, so why did we have to bring the subject up at all, let alone keep harping on with it... Somehow, the connection between brain and tongue gets disrupted, and stuff comes out of our mouths that's going to land us deep in the mire. No matter how hard we try to avoid references to obviously taboo subjects, Tourette's Troll is constantly fiddling with the circuits in our heads to make them the sole topics of conversation—and in the most offensive way possible. The best thing to do is to keep your mouth firmly shut, of course, but why should the foot-in-mouth fairy stop when he's enjoying himself? When Tourette's Troll takes over, you're in it up to your neck.

A tangled web...
Neurotransmitters woven into chaos are a specialty of this beast.

AFFILIATION
Secretary of the Guild of the Pixies of Perdition

MOST ACTIVE
When you've overslept, or when leaving the washroom

TEMPERAMENT
Forgetful and careless

Undone

Elder brother of the elegant Undine, Undone is the tramp of the family—unkempt, unwashed, and unpleasant. Not content with being negligent in his own affairs, though, he is meticulous in ensuring that we should suffer in a similar manner. Put simply, he undoes all those things we want to remain done up, and leaves undone those things that we thought we had done.

Principally interested in clothing, ugly brother Undone has a knack of untying shoelaces during tennis matches, unbuttoning blouses at the point of maximum exposure, and unzipping flies precisely as you leave the men's room, but can also unscrew bottle tops inside overloaded shopping bags and loosen the retaining screws on things such as bookshelves.

If only that were all. His favorite party trick consists of letting us ponder whether we've left things undone—switching the oven off, locking the front door, that sort of thing—then firmly instilling a nagging doubt as we fly away to our vacation destination.

AFFILIATION
Branch of the Ancient Order of
Failure to Communicate Fairies

MOST ACTIVE
In traffic jams

TEMPERAMENT
Bad-tempered and belligerent

HABITAT
All forms of road transport

CHARACTER
Really nasty—don't mess with these guys

KNOWN ASSOCIATIONS
Tourette's Troll, Moodshifting Meanies

Road Rage Goblins

Normally you're as mild-mannered as Clark Kent, content to let the world pass you by as you drive along, but Road Rage Goblins can change you into the Incredible Hulk in two seconds flat. How do they do that? I mean, it really doesn't matter that some guy has just jumped the line and cut in front of you, but it really gets to you. So what if that kid just clipped your side-view mirror as he passed on his bike? It's not broken! And there are plenty of spaces around, why is it you want to park just there where that blue car's gone in? The Road Rage Goblins, allegedly of Sicilian descent, magnify every minor irritation on our highways (road hogs, traffic jams, failure to signal, that sort of thing) and convince us that these misdemeanors are personal slights that must be viciously avenged.

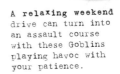

A relaxing weekend drive can turn into an assault course with these Goblins playing havoc with your patience.

59

CHAPTER FOUR

The Failure-to-Communicate Fairies

We notice the effects of the Failure to Communicate Fairies in our everyday inability to get our message across, get from A to B without incident, or find out what is really going on. Because they are so good at interfering with our communications infrastructures, we tend to forget just what geniuses of cooperation these fairy disrupters are.

Wherever information, goods, or people need to be sent from one place to another, these tireless workers of the Bad Fairy community can be found subtly disrupting everything that should make their passage smooth and uneventful. Not only do they wreak havoc on the mechanical and electrical means of communication—from telephone lines to car engines, e-mail connections to air traffic control—they also introduce a degree of human error into all our attempts to use these devices. Constantly offering us the wrong end of the stick, they ensure that we are given just the right amount of incorrect information, and that we will leap to the obviously wrong conclusion, or make ourselves disastrously misunderstood.

So, when you next find yourself incommunicado, incomprehensible, or in limbo somewhere, you'll appreciate how diligent the manipulators of miscommunication have been in their work.

AFFILIATION
Principal, the Fairy Institute
for Miscommunication

MOST ACTIVE
At formal presentations
and dinners

TEMPERAMENT
Cheerful, quick-witted

Slip o' the Tongue Fairy

It's not the long, difficult words that trip us up, it's the short everyday phrases that are the fertile ground in which the Slip o' the Tongue Fairy sows her seeds of disconnect. We know darn well what it is we want to say, but she makes sure that somehow, it just doesn't come out that way. All those minute errors of pronunciation, spoonerisms, and malapropisms tumble out, and would be amusing if they didn't have such dire consequences. When at the firm's dinner you thank your hosts for their hostility, raise your glass to the Queer old Dean, or announce that you really enjoy working in pubic relations, you know that Slip o' the Tongue has taken charge. Or maybe it's her Austrian cousin, the psychologist Freudian Slip, whose tricks include extracting habits out of rats… But in any case, once the words are out, it's best not to try to retract them, it will only leave you open for more mischief, at the mercy of this Bad Fairy.

Digging yourself into a hole?
Oops, once the words are out, there is no taking them back.

AFFILIATION
Curiously, a member of the
Guild of Bodily Function Fairies

MOST ACTIVE
Late at night, when
you're in the shower

TEMPERAMENT
Nervous and apologetic

HABITAT
Telephone exchanges,
and receivers

CHARACTER
Scatterbrained but
hardworking

KNOWN ASSOCIATIONS
Bad Timing Elves,
Insomnia

Wrong Number Fairy

A true mistress of the art of crossing wires, the Wrong Number Fairy wreaks maximum havoc with the minimum of effort by transposing digits deep within the telephone system, or simply guiding your finger to exactly the wrong button. Although it's really annoying to reach the local Chinese laundry every time you try to contact your office, it's even worse when you're on the receiving end. Still dripping from rushing out of the shower, you politely point out (for the third time today), that there is no Brett Startwinkle at this address. Later, just as you finally fall asleep at 3 A.M., you find yourself explaining just why it is that you haven't delivered the pizza to a town more than two hundred miles away. Leaving your answering machine on doesn't help—you end up phoning back to make the same explanations—on your bill.

Telephone traumas
A seemingly innocent telephone can become an evil weapon.

AFFILIATION
Secretary of the Guild of Fairy
Communication Workers

MOST ACTIVE
When you really need
to get somewhere

TEMPERAMENT
Slow and unreliable

Timetable Troll

10.32
11.05
24.02
07.55

It should be quite simple. The timetable is there to tell us when the train, bus or plane leaves and arrives, and where it stops. But the Timetable Troll introduces complications, exceptions, footnotes and small print that make it impossible for even professors of logistics to understand. Introducing illogical page turns, subtly changing the information, and removing cross-references and asterisks, this malevolent devil is responsible for transport misery worldwide. It doesn't matter how carefully you've studied the arcane details of the traveler's bible, the Timetable Troll can still make sure you get to the station just in time to see your train leaving (it leaves one minute earlier on alternate Tuesdays), or arrive to find you've got seven hours to kill until the next connection. When all else fails, he'll instigate a transit workers' strike, so you're not going anywhere.

18.52

Checking your watch
...won't guarantee
that you'll get to
that final destination.

AFFILIATION
Coopted on to the Guild of the Pixies of Perdition

MOST ACTIVE
During the holiday season

TEMPERAMENT
A first-class administrator

HABITAT
All forms of transport

CHARACTER
Intellectual, in an absent-minded professor way

KNOWN ASSOCIATIONS
*Translocation Fairy,
Timetable Troll*

The Lost Luggage Leprechaun

Breakfast in London, dinner in New York, luggage in Kuala Lumpur. Looks like your baggage handling ticket has been meddled with by the Translocation Fairy. The Lost Luggage Leprechaun lurks in every bag you pack, and makes sure that wherever you are going, it isn't. Wave goodbye to your belongings at check-in, it's going to be a long time until you meet again. And hang on to your hand luggage, too—he operates a special kind of trap door into limbo from inside the compartment above your head, and delights in sending passports, cameras, and insurance documents to entirely different destinations. Although he is best known for his work on major airlines, he doesn't confine his mischief to air travel—the lost property departments of railways, bus companies, and taxi services are testimony to his versatility. You wouldn't believe what he deposits in these places. Or maybe you would.

Hours of waiting
If your bag is the last one out, count yourself lucky.

69

AFFILIATION
The Ancient Order of Failure
to Communicate Fairies

MOST ACTIVE
In the corridors of power

TEMPERAMENT
Obstinate and awkward

Will o' the Whispers

The quintessential Failure to Communicate Fairy, Will o' the Whispers prides himself on turning the most innocent conversation into a rumor that will grow into a diplomatic incident and even bring down governments. He's a sort of simultaneous mistranslator between the speaker and listener, introducing inaccuracies and ambiguities and generally making sure that we all talk at cross-purposes. A simple device such as a noisy party, bad telephone line, or slight hearing loss will ensure that innocuous statements are misheard or misunderstood, and names are changed to incriminate the innocent—how were you to know that there are two guys named John Smith? Will also activates the network that sets the ball rolling, instilling an irresistible urge to pass on the misinformation, introducing further errors into the retelling of your story, and exaggerating it beyond all recognition in the process, so that anybody hearing it will jump to exactly the wrong conclusion.

Canal capers...
Did he say you need a "cute tick" for your ear?

71

Breakdown Brownies

It's been a long day, and you're on your way home, through the horrific traffic that held you up for hours. It's cold and rainy, and it's midnight. That's when the Breakdown Brownies are most likely to strike. For no apparent reason, the car dies on you. It just won't start again, probably because they've disconnected a vital component deep inside the engine, just behind that complicated thing so you can't see or get at it. Soaked and freezing, you eventually manage to coax the engine back to life, when you notice the flat tire that was perfectly okay only a moment ago. No matter, you've got a spare. And you have kept that properly inflated, haven't you? Oh well, never mind. This is where the cell phone would come in handy—if only you'd charged the battery. The pay phone is under the control of the Wrong Number Fairy, but by 4 A.M. you can rest assured the breakdown service is on its way, with only another six hours to wait.

One after the other
When your car breaks down it will seem that everything breaks down, leaving you totally disabled.

73

AFFILIATION
Associate Executive members of all Bad Fairy Groups

MOST ACTIVE
Just when you thought it was safe

TEMPERAMENT
Malicious, calculating, not easily distracted

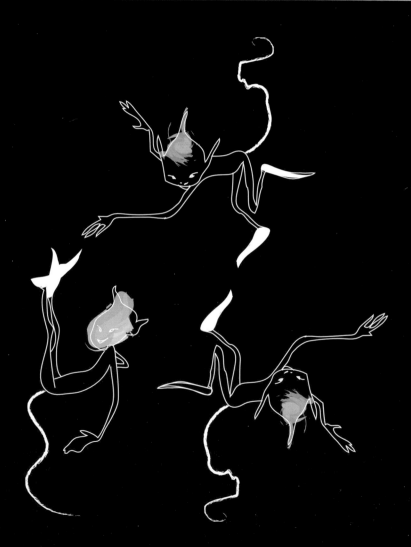

Bad Timing Elves

When the phone rings, just as you sink into a hot tub, who are you going to blame? Right—the Bad Timing Elves, the patron saints of unhappy coincidence. These little guys know exactly the right moment to cause most embarrassment, and do so with startling frequency. In addition to causing their own brand of jolly mayhem, they work as a team to provide information to other Fairy Folk regarding when best (or worst) to play their pranks. Ever wonder why there's a lull in the conversation in the restaurant precisely when you relieve the pressure of internal gases? Or why you reveal your innermost thoughts about the person who has just arrived behind you? Now you know. It was one of those pesky little varmints—but how do they do it? Some say that they just have an innate sense of precisely the wrong moment, others believe they work with phenomenally accurate chronometers of their own devising. Whatever the methods, they are the critters who set the timetable for the rest of us.

Time to relax?
You can guarantee it won't last more than a second.

CHAPTER FIVE

The Domestic Demons

You probably think the word "homesick" describes that feeling you have when you're away and think longingly of your dear home. Well, there's an army of sprites, brownies, and various Domestic Demons who give a whole new meaning to the word. They work their magic on every nook and crevice of your home to make it truly sick.

Most worryingly, they have units devoted to slowly but surely attacking the fabrics of our homes; turning that dream house, fabulous apartment or great little bachelor pad into a building site where the more work is done, the more the professionals uncover expensive problems. Bricks and mortar, woodwork, plumbing, electrical, heating—you name it, they've thought of a way to make it go wrong.

Not content to leave it at that, however, the Domestic Demons have other tricks up their capacious sleeves. They'll find a way to make life within your household more interesting than you'd bargained for. Their control over everything from your domestic appliances to your household pets is total, and guarantees that you won't be able to come home from work to a restful, relaxing environment. Oh no. You've got a constant list of little things that need doing around the house, and the threat of one or two major jobs too.

AFFILIATION
Guild of Domestic and
Catering Fairies

MOST ACTIVE
While you're preparing
for guests

TEMPERAMENT
Airy-fairy, artistic
and creative

HABITAT
Nooks and crannies

CHARACTER
Endearing, but unattractive in
the personal hygiene department

KNOWN ASSOCIATIONS
Infestation Imps, Miasma

Cobweb

Housework...don't you just love it? Well, it has to be done, and there is at least some satisfaction in having a clean and tidy environment. But where does all that dirt come from? I mean, you never see any spiders, so where do their webs come from? And what about all that dust? Not to mention the horrible stuff that builds up behind the kitchen appliances (please don't mention that). Of course, you know where it all really comes from. There must be a bad fairy responsible—and there is—Cobweb. Traditionally, she was thought of as one of the prettiest of all the fairy folk, but the reality is unfortunately more disgusting. She is always one step ahead of you in your housekeeping, no matter how meticulous you are, and from her store of repulsive substances, she can produce a huge dangling web to hover over your guest's plate at dinner, conjure up something truly unpleasant in the ice you put in his gin and tonic, or blow a huge dust bunny out from under the fridge.

Magnifying mysteries
No matter how thorough you are with your cleaning, dirt and cobwebs will pop up in no time.

79

AFFILIATION
Health Officer, Guild of
Domestic and Catering Fairies

MOST ACTIVE
Just after shopping sprees or
trips to the cleaners

TEMPERAMENT
Flighty, but stubborn

HABITAT
Wardrobes, drying racks,
washing machines

CHARACTER
Attractive but destructive

KNOWN ASSOCIATIONS
Infestation Imps, Undone

Moth

Another one of those fairies whose name belies her evil intent, Moth may look pretty enough in her immaculate diaphanous outfit, but boy, can she make a mess of your clothes. You thought she just made holes in your best sweaters—well, that's only one of her neat party tricks. She's a genius when it comes to all kinds of fabrics, the exact opposite of Cinderella's fairy godmother, and can turn a stunning ball gown into rags. Using her own special potions, she makes holes, fades colors, shrinks fabrics, and weakens button threads, then sits back and watches the fun as you discover your entire wardrobe is unwearable. Moth is also the little stinker behind that embarrassing stain on the seat of your pants, and the way your laundry has all turned out pink (except the pink things, of course). Also, she doesn't restrict herself to clothing—bed linens, towels, and chair coverings all come under her jurisdiction.

Household pet(s)
As quickly as fungi grows on out-of-date food, Moth can turn your prized wardrobe into rags.

AFFILIATION
Guild of Domestic Fairy Farm
Operatives

MOST ACTIVE
In hot and humid weather

TEMPERAMENT
Patient and caring

Infestation Imps

When it comes to husbandry and horticulture, these guys are unequalled in the fairy world. They tend to their flocks of woodworms, termites, cockroaches, rats, and mice, and cultivate huge fields of dry rot and various fungi just to make home ownership more interesting. There isn't a substance known to man that isn't used as fertilizer for their crops, nor a human habitation that doesn't also serve as pasture for their herds. The Infestation Imps strike right at the heart of your happy home, reducing it to powder before your eyes, and disproving the old adage "as safe as houses." And if they can't actually bring your house down around your ears, they can populate it with the less attractive four-, six-, and eight-legged creatures that most of us would rather not even dream about. Of course, you won't discover that your home is part of a fairy agricultural complex until it's too late—you've moved in with them.

Creepy and crawly
These imps are often invisible to the human eye, but you know they are up to no good.

83

AFFILIATION
Fellow of the Fairy Institute of
Mechanical Engineering

MOST ACTIVE
At the first signs of hunger
and thirst

TEMPERAMENT
Obstinate and unforgiving

HABITAT
Every cupboard in the house

CHARACTER
Ingenious and inventive

KNOWN ASSOCIATIONS
Gremlins

Bottle-Top Bogey

Like most other Domestic Demons, the Bottle-Top Bogey has a scientific rather than an artistic bent. In fact, his laboratory is devoted to the exploration of just one physical property: adhesion. Chemicals developed at his bench are applied to jars and bottles, making their tops almost impossible to remove—I say almost, because the most fiendish thing about these adhesives is that when they do give way they do so suddenly, showering the person trying to get in with the entire contents of the bottle. Other products from the same lab include the fragile ring-pull that comes away before the can is open, the keyed fish or meat tin that tears into lethally jagged edges, and the ubiquitous plastic wrapping that just can't be ripped off. But what has to be his masterpiece of malign design is the cardboard drink container, with the deceptively inviting instruction to "tear here to open."

An innocent can top?
Don't be fooled by practicality, this ring-pull should carry a health warning.

85

AFFILIATION
Associate Member of the Elfin Sound Engineers Union

MOST ACTIVE
Exclusively at night

TEMPERAMENT
Extrovert, musical

HABITAT
Bedrooms and corridors

CHARACTER
Articulate but mournful

KNOWN ASSOCIATIONS
Insomnia, Infestation Imps,
the Alarm Afreet

Creaking Floorboard Banshee

Thanks to Insomnia, there are often times when we lie awake at night, listening to the silence, and begin to worry. And as these fears grow into full-blown dread, that's when it happens. Was that an intruder, or was it just the cat? Actually, neither. It's the Creaking Floorboard Banshee, the patron fairy of things that go bump in the night—leaving you quaking in bed. Sometimes, though, she is not so much scary as annoying, keeping you just out of reach of sleep with that dripping tap that you can't be bothered to get out of bed to fix, or the squeaky bedspring that wakes you each time you nod off. Best of all is her most subtle trick— absolute silence. Suddenly, she'll make a noise that didn't happen that will still wake you up screaming "Wassallanoisabouden?" or something similar.

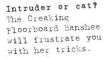

Intruder or cat?
The Creaking
Floorboard Banshee
will frustrate you
with her tricks.

AFFILIATION
*Life President of the Guild of
Bad Fairy Parfumiers*

MOST ACTIVE
High summer

TEMPERAMENT
Ethereal and other-worldly

HABITAT
*Drains, toilets, and
under floors*

CHARACTER
*Insidious and difficult
to ignore*

KNOWN ASSOCIATIONS
*Infestation Imps, Partypooper
Fairy, Stinkerbell*

Miasma

They say that a good way to sell a property is to brew
coffee while showing prospective buyers around. Sounds like a
good idea to me, if only to disguise the effects that Miasma has had on
your home. She's the fairy responsible for all the unpleasant odors, from
nasty whiffs to gut-wrenchingly ghastly stenches that are the downside
of modern conveniences such as drains, toilets, and refrigerators. Often
working in collaboration with the Infestation Imps, she can plant
somewhere inaccessible a dead or decaying something
(you really don't want to know what) that gradually
makes its presence felt throughout the whole
house. Blocked drains are an obvious ploy to
create a little olfactory mayhem, but she's also
capable of less blatant tactics. Who knows what's
causing that funny smell that you can't quite
locate, somewhere down in the basement? And it
definitely seems to be getting worse, doesn't it?

A nose inspection...
... is what you'll need
to do to track down
the smelly work of
this Bad Fairy.

AFFILIATION
Animal Division, Guild of
Domestic Fairy Farm Operatives

MOST ACTIVE
The living room—especially on
soft furnishings

TEMPERAMENT
Love me, love my dog

HABITAT
Dog baskets, cat trays

CHARACTER
A faithful friend
(too faithful, actually)

KNOWN ASSOCIATIONS
Partypooper Fairy, Infestation
Imps, Cobweb

The Cat Sick Sprite

A lot of people think that no home is complete without some animal companionship, and there are a lot of fairies who would agree wholeheartedly—in particular, the Cat Sick Sprite. He realizes how much unconditional love we show our pets, and feels we should have something in return. Trouble is, his idea of fair repayment isn't necessarily the same as ours. At the top of the list are fleas, ticks, and other fellow travelers that our four-legged friends bring home with them and unselfishly share with us. Also, they are generous in spreading their coats during the molting season (all year round in most cases), and of course, the hairballs that give this sprite his name. Other gifts he prompts them to give us include dead birds and rodents, but it is really in the field of incontinence that he makes us realize the true joys of pet ownership.

CHAPTER SIX

The Rude Mechanicals

Some of the most ancient of the Fairy Guilds were established to deal with the labor-saving devices that humans so optimistically invented. Did I say labor-saving? The Rude Mechanicals have other ideas. Whenever we come up with an idea designed to make life easier, they introduce a few snags to make it twice as difficult.

There are significantly more of them these days, as we have so many more gadgets and gizmos, but they've been around for an awfully (and I mean awfully) long time. Since the discovery of fire, and the simultaneous discovery of burns, they've been making us rue the day we stumbled across the concept of technology. Early successes include the invention of the wobbly wheel, which is still in use today in supermarket carts, and that perennial favorite, the loose hammer head.

So now you know. The next time you get tempted by the Shopping Siren to part with your hard-earned cash in return for the latest state-of-the-art, must-have indispensable household help, rest assured that not only will it not do what it was intended to (and you could have done the job in half the time), but it's quite likely to cause more trouble than it solves, thanks to the Rude Mechanicals.

AFFILIATION
Associate Members of all
Mechanical Fairy Guilds

MOST ACTIVE
When you are completely at
the mercy of technology

TEMPERAMENT
Painstaking and meticulous

HABITAT
In anything mechanical
or electrical

CHARACTER
Not actually evil, just irksome

KNOWN ASSOCIATIONS
Breakdown Brownies, Three
Gleeful Sisters of Contrariness

Gremlins

The most ubiquitous of all the Rude Mechanicals, Gremlins are much more than the mere tinkerers that they appear to be. They are highly trained master craftsmen, the cream of the technicians, and engineers of the Fairy community. Many of them are specialists in their particular fields, lavishing their talents on clocks, locks, and domestic appliances, or applying the latest technology to throw a spanner into the workings of microchips and smart cards. Their skill in all things technical explains why, when you rely on any piece of equipment, it's bound to let you down. From the kitchen timer that, in conjunction with your oven, tells you when your dinner is nicely burnt, to the ATM that swallows your card and then tells you you have a massive overdraft, or the self-assembly furniture that resists all attempts to put together, Gremlins are continually making their presence felt.

Cell phone gone completely dead? Then you know a Gremlin is at work.

95

AFFILIATION
*Honorary member, Institute of
Electrical Elves*

MOST ACTIVE
In the race to deadlines

TEMPERAMENT
Cranky beyond belief

HABITAT
Inside computers, palm pilots, and calculators

CHARACTER
Surprisingly infuriating

KNOWN ASSOCIATIONS
Gremlins, Bad Timing Elves

PC Blossom

A true specialist, this relative of the Gremlin works exclusively in the realm of computers and connected devices. She inhabits the inner workings of your computer, sending electronic messages to all peripherals that will have you on to the help line in no time at all. Sure, you know all about viruses and hackers infiltrating your system, and you've bought all the protection they can sell you, but there's no known antidote to PC Blossom. Irritating little things such as adding spam to your email inbox, flashing incomprehensible error messages, or sending confusing messages to your printer are her trademark moves, but

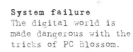

System failure
The digital world is made dangerous with the tricks of PC Blossom.

when she pulls out all the stops, the results can be truly catastrophic. Essential files can suddenly disappear from your hard drive, applications can refuse to open, or best of all, a complete system can crash. And you didn't back up your files like you know you should, did you?

97

AFFILIATION
Press Officer, the Gnome
Council for New Technology

MOST ACTIVE
During the last episode of
anything on TV

TEMPERAMENT
Well adjusted, focused

Aerial

Like PC Blossom, Aerial is a comparatively modern Bad Fairy who restricts her activities to interfering in our enjoyment of television. Recently, she has branched out into the allied field of VCRs and DVDs, and even the stereo, but it's the moving wallpaper in the corner of the room where she shows her real talents. For instance, how come you can receive channel three perfectly, but not channel four? Or, with a little adjustment to the tuning, exactly the other way around? It's Aerial at work, turning the screen into an image of a gray wall in a snowstorm, with the soundtrack from the middle of a hurricane. And why did we record two hours of Siberian poetry recitals instead of that film we wanted to watch? It must be the work of Aerial. Another of her irksome pranks is to run down the batteries in the remote control. Wait a minute, where has the remote control gone?

Quit cursing...
... the pirate radio stations, you know who's really jinxed the airwaves.

99

AFFILIATION
*Board Member of all
Mechanical Fairy Guilds*

MOST ACTIVE
In extremes of temperature

TEMPERAMENT
*Slow to react, but watch out
when he does*

HABITAT
Plumbing, heating, and cooling appliances

CHARACTER
Can only be pushed so far

KNOWN ASSOCIATIONS
Partypooper Fairy, Gremlins

The Thermostat Troll

I used to wonder how the stuff I put in the fridge could be kept at exactly the right temperature to make it a breeding ground for noxious bacteria and that soft, gray, hairy mold. That was before I discovered the Thermostat Troll. A real wizard when it comes to temperature control, he recalibrates the thermostats on all our household machines, taking them to extremes of Fahrenheit and Celcius that you didn't know existed. Food in the freezer reaches absolute zero and becomes a collection of unrecognizable snowballs, and the oven is turned into a domestic charcoal burner. Heating, particularly in public transport, only kicks in during a heatwave, and remains resolutely Arctic throughout the winter months. As for the bathroom—well, guess who controls the tiny distance on the shower knob between icy cold and scalding hot, and can change its position at random during your daily shower?

The Troll keeps you on your toes, as you hop from foot to foot.

101

AFFILIATION
*Institute of Electrical Elves,
Lighting Division*

MOST ACTIVE
*Mainly nocturnal, but diurnal
during bad weather*

TEMPERAMENT
A real bright spark

The Genie of the Lamp

Yes, it does say 100 watts on the box, but when you switch the light on it's so dim it almost makes the room darker—unlike the other three that won't light at all. That's thanks to the Genie of the Lamp, a.k.a. Jill o' Lantern. Many hands make light work, they say, but her nimble fingers are constantly employed to make sure the light doesn't work. She personally oversees the production of every light bulb to ensure the filament has the correct amount of built-in obsolescence, and regulates the rate at which they deteriorate so that every lamp in the house will blow within minutes of one another. And when you go to replace them, you'll find she's exchanged your stock of bayonet-capped bulbs with screw-tops (or vice versa). Maybe it's not the bulb, though, it could be the main fuse in the cellar. Now, why won't that darn flashlight work?

Aladdin should count...
...himself lucky this particular genie was on vacation.

MOST ACTIVE
When you've got nothing better
to do with your time

Gadget Gnomes

From the moment he purchases his first multi-purpose army knife, the one with all the attachments for doing practical things like removing horses from boy scouts' hooves, the Gadget Gnomes have got the average man hooked on gizmos. Women are less susceptible, of course, but they don't get off lightly either—have a look at the average hair and beauty salon. But it's the guys who really go overboard, hypnotized by the ads for the latest time-saving tool or executive toy. How did we ever manage without ear and nose hair trimmers? Or electric card shufflers? Or motorized necktie caddies? Why did we ever buy them? And how come they never work like they do in the commercials? Gadget Gnomes persuade us that they're indispensable, then prove that they're also incapable of doing the job for which they were designed. Especially if you can't find a supplier of the correct size batteries (not included).

Another pen knife?
You're kidding yourself that this one has new essential bits.

105

AFFILIATION
Association of Nocturnal
Fairy Operatives

MOST ACTIVE
The hours of darkness

TEMPERAMENT
Mercurial and mysterious

HABITAT
Around any disaster-activated device

CHARACTER
Gleefully mischievous

KNOWN ASSOCIATIONS
Breakdown Brownies, Insomnia

The Alarm Afreet

The Alarm Afreet leads an almost exclusively nocturnal existence, noiselessly darting around densely populated areas in his quest for electronic surveillance devices to disturb. Once he's found one, he'll take a minute to catch his breath, leaning on an alarmed car until it screams across the whole neighborhood, or pensively snatching a puff on his pipe beneath the smoke alarm in a block of apartments. If he's lucky, he'll find an unoccupied property next door to a family of light sleepers, and manage to fool them into believing they're being burgled. Most of these ploys result in the appearance of emergency vehicles, sirens wailing, and he can relax in the knowledge of a job well done. Sometimes, just for a change, he'll do some daytime work, and get an entire office building evacuated by leaving an unmarked package in the lobby containing a loudly ticking alarm clock.

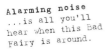

Alarming noise
...is all you'll hear when this Bad Fairy is around.

CHAPTER SEVEN

The Time-of-Your-Life Fairies

For each stage of life, there is a Bad Fairy looking out for us. Once the Fairy Badmother has left the newborn's bedside, the Time-of-Your-Life Fairies grab the baton and pass it on, so that every period you go through, whatever your age, has its own peculiar problems.

Right through infancy, these fairies look for opportunities to be irksome: from teething through childhood diseases to the everyday knocks, scrapes and playtime frustrations, they make themselves known. Then, onto schooldays, "the best days of your life"—which is either a downright lie or just something to make the rest of your existence look unwelcoming. Plus, we have the joys of Pubertiana's attentions, whose effects can linger on until we start our own families and the cycle starts again.

But the Bad Fairies won't let us off even after our kids have flown the nest. Oh no. Middle age is when they really start having fun. From here, our bodies, like retiring college professors, lose their faculties. Slowly but surely, we all pass our prime—some of us miss it altogether—and start to grow old disgracefully. And just before we shuffle off our mortal rockers, we are treated to a period when we lament the fact that the anguish of youth is wasted on the young.

AFFILIATION	MOST ACTIVE	TEMPERAMENT
Student Members, Young	Up to the age of discretion	Studious, but easily distracted
Troublemakers Union	(whenever that is)	

HABITAT
The nursery, crèche, and playschool

CHARACTER
Playful and immature

KNOWN ASSOCIATIONS
Bodily Function Fairies,
Moodshifting Meanies

The Little People's Little People

The training ground for Bad Fairies is provided by apprenticeships monitored by all the Bad Fairy Guilds, and the majority of young imps and sprites learn their trade as Little People's Little People. Here, they can practice their art and perfect their skills by inflicting delights such as nappy rash, colic, inconsolable howling, and crankiness on their young victims, and gradually work their way through to more complex tasks as they grow up. After a few months of fairly simple stuff, they can move up to the more satisfying annoyances of teething and bedwetting, and work out their own strategies for inducing uncontrollable tantrums—all under the watchful eye of their Guild Mentor. At this point, they are encouraged to find a specialty that suits them, and then the nurseries, playschools, and crèches of the human world provide an ideal environment in which they can experiment.

Little People...
... but with lots of commanding power to meddle in our lives.

AFFILIATION
*Education Officer, the Union of
Apprenticed Imps*

MOST ACTIVE
Around adolescents

TEMPERAMENT
Sooo not hip, you know. Totally.

HABITAT
Under your skin

CHARACTER
Uncool, or what? Like,
get a life.

KNOWN ASSOCIATIONS
Zitania, Moodshifting Meanies

Pubertiana

The time eventually comes to all of us when we must put childish things behind us, and Pubertiana is always there to lend a helping hand. To guarantee that the passage from childhood to adulthood is not a smooth one, she works closely with Mother Nature so that just when the pressure is really on at school with exams and career choices, the hormones will kick in big time. Boys sprout hair in unexpected places, and swing between booming baritone and squeaking treble, and girls develop puppy fat, bumps, and awkward times of the month. Pubertiana causes both sexes embarrassment and misery with zits, sweats, and blushing, and instills into all adolescents an interest in the mechanics of procreation—but prevents them from exploring this by blatantly affecting their ability to communicate with the opposite sex in anything but giggles or unintelligible grunts. Just to make matters worse, throughout this period, she also turns their parents into hideous, unfair losers.

Buy in bulk
That pimple cream won't have the cap on for any extended period of time.

113

AFFILIATION
Chief Executive Officer,
Commission for Human Sprites

MOST ACTIVE
Around women of an uncertain
age

TEMPERAMENT
Changeable, inclined to blow
hot and cold

HABITAT
Public places, shops, and restaurants

CHARACTER
Actually quite amiable, and modest

KNOWN ASSOCIATIONS
The Failure to Communicate Fairies

The Invisibility Fairy

By throwing her cloak over her victim, and with a wave of her little wand, the Invisibility Fairy can make anybody seem to disappear. But, being of a certain age herself, she usually chooses to bestow her gift on women in early middle-age. As far as anybody whose attention they are seeking is concerned, they suddenly cease to exist. In the store trying to complain, standing on the bus next to a seated teenager, or attempting to cross a busy street, they become as transparent as a plate glass window. It's no good shouting, either, because the Invisibility Fairy can also reduce the perceived sound of women's voices to less than a whisper, especially in public or when talking to her husband. As an exception to her strangely sexist rule, she does now and again throw a veil over a middle-aged man, just for a change, usually when he's in a bar or restaurant trying to catch the waiter's eye.

No use checking for your reflection in the mirror.

115

AFFILIATION
Guild of the Bodily Function Fairies

MOST ACTIVE
When you think you're in your prime (i.e., just past it)

TEMPERAMENT
Subtle and insidious

HABITAT
In printing presses and optometrists' workshops

CHARACTER
A sort of indefinite article

KNOWN ASSOCIATIONS
Timetable Troll and Failure to Communicate Fairies

Myopina

The symptoms of incipient old age are many and varied, the most obvious being the strange feeling that the floor is no longer within easy reach, and the legs of chairs have been shortened. Of course, it's not your faculties that are failing—I mean, it's a known fact that young people mumble indistinctly—and Myopina does her bit to disrupt the smooth passage into senility. Although your eyesight is as good as ever, she goes around changing the type size in telephone directories, shrinking maps and diagrams, and closing up the eyes of needles so that you get the impression you need to visit the optician more regularly. But beware— even if you get yourself a new pair of bifocals, Myopina is ready with her toolkit to regrind the lenses making them effectively useless. And if you peer over them, you'll find that you can't quite get the book far enough from your eyes to focus properly. It seems she's mysteriously shortened your arms as well.

New glasses?
Unfortunately, these won't make a blind bit of difference.

117

AFFILIATION
Past President (retired), the Ancient Order of Elvish Thing

MOST ACTIVE
Mainly in later life, but can strike at any time

TEMPERAMENT
Endearing but slightly dotty

Tip o' the Tongue

Also known as Aphasia (or is it Amnesia? I forget), Tip o' the Tongue visits us all once we reach a certain age. Snatching thoughts as they make their way from our brains to our mouths, she ensures we suddenly find ourselves totally unable to recall the name of our best friend, or incapable of bringing to mind the word for that thingamajig that we use for, you know, doing whatchercallit. Worse still, once you start trying to remember, your mind becomes a complete blank and you lose track of the subject of the conversation altogether. It's all thanks to Tip o' the Tongue tinkering with our mental wotsits. Useless information leaps to the fore—Cary Grant's real name, for instance*— but your own telephone number? No, don't tell me, it's, erm … there's a seven in it, no, hang on, sorry, what was the question again?

*Archibald Leach

Frustration?
Hardly a strong enough word for what you'll be feeling.

AFFILIATION

Most Senior Associate in the Congress of Dwarf Elders

MOST ACTIVE

When all else fails. Exactly—when all else fails completely

TEMPERAMENT

Relentless and unforgiving

Wrinklestiltskin

After a lifetime of suffering the vicissitudes of the Bad Fairies, you might think they'd let up for a while. Sadly, you'd be mistaken. As we settle into well-earned retirement, that gnarled and malevolent old dwarf Wrinklestiltskin takes over where the others left off. Overnight, he attacks our metabolisms to remind us that our bodies are not our own. Despite the increase in rumblings and gurglings, digestive processes are not as efficient as they were, and our ability to burn off calories decreases alarmingly, at the same time as the extra flesh loses its natural resistance to gravity. As if that weren't enough, Wrinklestiltskin artistically carves free-form crow's feet into your face, redesigns knuckles, and decorates your extremities with normally invisible blood vessels, moles, and odd-colored spots, then leaves his luggage under your eyes. And you've still got years of minor ailments to look forward to, not to mention nose-dripping, dribbling, and incontinence. No really, please don't mention them.

Watch out!
Wrinklestiltskin's luggage will appear from nowhere, right under your eyes.

Genealogy

How they're all related

There is much confusion regarding the ancestry of the Bad Fairies, making it difficult to chart their genealogy and how bad stuff is passed on from age to age. This is why the Ancient Guilds of Fairy Craftsmen have become so important—because they provide the means of passing on Bad Fairy culture from generation to generation. Hence the emphasis in this book on the affiliations of the various Bad Fairy workers, rather than an exhaustive study of their ancestry.

So, with little known about the relationships of the Bad Fairies, it is impossible to tell who are the parents of, say, the Three Gleeful Sisters of Contrariness. We know they are indeed sisters, but there is some doubt as to their folks—most likely they are the daughters of Puck and The Fairy Badmother, but this was undoubtedly an illicit liaison (not uncommon among fairies). We're on more certain ground when it comes to the Fairies of the Darkside Division, as they are usually closely related to their better-documented Good Fairy counterparts. Robin Badfellow, Stinkerbell, and Undone are all the black sheep of their virtuous families, and Forget-Me-Not, Cobweb, and Moth have all strayed from the paths their parents laid down for them. So you can see just how difficult it is to document an accurate history—and equally impossible to avoid these irritating Bad Fairies from playing with our lives.

Elves, Dwarves, Gnomes, Pixies, and so on make up the vast majority of the so-called Bad Fairies examined in this little book. But because they live in "free spirit" communes on ancient tribal lines, where there is a collective responsibility for the upbringing of children and a rather cavalier attitude toward monogamy, it's virtually impossible to pinpoint who begat whom, and—because of their startling longevity—when. The most we can say is that interbreeding between the various groups is rare, so each "tribe" (Elves, Dwarves, Gnomes, Pixies, etc.) forms an extended family unit, separate from the others and with its own characteristics and culture. In the case of the Trolls, this has caused some problems of incestuous inbreeding, but (so far) without affecting their work.

More research into this fascinating and confusing area is obviously called for, and is unfortunately beyond the scope of this preliminary study. Fairies, by nature elusive and ethereal, are a notoriously tough bunch to categorize, and despite their all-too-frequent intrusions into our lives, we have precious few opportunities to delve into theirs. Nevertheless, we should not let this lack of solid information about their private lives persuade us that they don't wreak havoc on ours— still less that they just don't exist. I can assure you, they do.

Glossary

An A–Z of Bad Fairy terms

AFREET

An evil demon of Arabic descent, found increasingly all over the world. The best known is the Alarm Afreet, but there are Afreets in all the major Bad Fairy Guilds.

BOGEY

For a long time, the Bogey was the "village idiot" among the gnomes and dwarves, but is not so much stupid as downright evil.

CHANGELING

A human abducted by Bad Fairies as a child. Changelings are seldom admitted as full members of the Guilds, but can be useful in providing inside information.

DWARF

Subterranean workers of the Bad Fairy underworld. They are unattractive little guys, and have enough chips on their shoulders to feed an army.

ELF

Good-looking, often glamorous, the elves are the jet-setters of the fairy community. Normally middle management or higher, they dominate the executive branches of the Fairy Guilds.

FAIRY

The generic term for all the little people of the spirit underworld. They come in all shapes and sizes, and control every aspect of human lives, good, bad, and indifferent.

GENIE or JINN

Related to the Afreet, and also from the Middle East. While the Good Fairy sector grants wishes to humans, the Bad ones make us wish they hadn't.

GNOME

Cheerful, rustic fairy folk with a well-developed sense of humor. They are the most likely candidates for the fairies said to live at the bottom of the garden.

GOBLIN or HOBGOBLIN

Practical jokers par excellence, goblins are responsible for the many little things that let us down. They are also infamous for their poor fashion sense.

IMP

A young Bad Fairy. Many imps are apprentices in the Bad Fairy Guilds and the thriving Young Troublemakers Union keeps them out of—sorry, into—mischief.

KREMLIN

Probably a misprint for Gremlin, one of the more mischievous of the Gnome community, with an affinity for things mechanical.

LEPRECHAUN

The Irish branch of the Elf family, traditionally blessed with the gift of the gab and an idiosyncratic brand of logic.

MUSHROOMS (AND TOADSTOOLS)

Long associated with fairy folk, they are believed by humans to have some mystical significance. Fairies, however, consider them simply delicious.

NOAM CHOMSKY

Despite his name, Mr. Chomsky is an American thinker and writer who has, as far as I know, no connection with the fairy world.

OVERWORLD
See UNDERWORLD.

PIXIE or PIXY
The smallest of the fairies, but no less efficient in mischief-making. Pixies have the reputation of being lucky, in the same way as horseshoes that are dropped on your head.

QUARK
A subatomic particle that physicists insist exists and explains some strange phenomena—but we know who's really responsible, don't we?

SPRITES and BROWNIES
Household spirits who look after every aspect of our homes, but whose Darkside members are dedicated to domestic mayhem.

TROLL
An ugly, slow-witted creature with unfortunate eating habits, halitosis, and very poor people skills—hence usually restricted to administrative work.

UNDERWORLD
See OVERWORLD.

VICTIM
That's us. The butt of the Bad Fairies' humor, and fall guy in their Machiavellian schemes.

WAND
Indispensable item of fairy equipment, waved at every opportunity. Has the power to transform everyday objects into lethal mantraps.

XYLOPHONE
Nothing to do with fairies at all, but appears in nearly every A–Z.

YGGDRASIL
The ash tree in Norse mythology connecting heaven, earth, and hell—a really important concept in fairy folklore. No, really, it is.

ZILCH
The sum total of words to do with fairies I could find beginning with the letter Z.

Index

Acknowledgments

I am indebted to many people for their help in producing this little book—
not least the goodest fairy of them all, Vivienne—but also the legion of little
helpers who kept all the Bad Fairies at bay while I worked and who prefer to
remain nameless (they know who they are). Thanks are also due to the Ivy
Press for believing in me even if they didn't (initially) believe in fairies.

Getty-Images: 27 Ray Massey/Stone; 35 Ffoto Fictions/Taxi; 45 Tony
Garcia/Stone; 63 Larry Dale Gordon/The Image Bank; 73 Andre Gallant/The
Image Bank; 73 V.C.L/The Image Bank; 107 Daniel Arsenault/The Image Bank;
111 Stephanie Rausser/Taxi; 113 Trujillo-Paumier/The Image Bank; 115 Sean
Justice/Taxi; 119 Daniel Arsenault/Taxi; 121 Daly & Newton/The Image Bank.